DANNY A. NELMS AND
THOMAS F. MAHAN

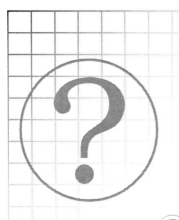

The
Why Factor

WINNING WITH WORKFORCE INTELLIGENCE

WESTBOW
PRESS
A DIVISION OF THOMAS NELSON

WestBow Press books may be ordered through booksellers or by contacting:

WestBow Press
A Division of Thomas Nelson
1663 Liberty Drive
Bloomington, IN 47403
www.westbowpress.com
1-(866) 928-1240

Certain stock imagery © Thinkstock.

ISBN: 978-1-4497-3957-7 (sc)
ISBN: 978-1-4497-3959-1 (e)

Library of Congress Control Number: 2012902000

Printed in the United States of America

WestBow Press rev. date: 2/20/2012

Dedication

To those organizations that strive to provide an environment where employees can truly realize their occupational purpose.

Contents

Foreword

In 2004 I met Dr. Tom Mahan, and he helped forever change the way I looked at the business world. Tom introduced me to the term "evidence-based management" and gave me a *Harvard Business Review* (Jan, 2006) article by Jeffrey Pfeffer and Robert Sutton, explaining the details of this still widely unknown management principle.

As a business-focused human resource professional, I began to question and re-evaluate many of the traditional management practices that I viewed as burdensome, expensive, and ineffective. I came to believe that we were (mostly) doing things because it was how we had always done them. Like most managers, I seemed to fall right in line with all of the best sellers of the day and longstanding practices professed to be the right way to manage human behavior.

Ongoing conversations with Dr. Mahan challenged me to develop a new way of thinking about human behavior in the workplace. To be fair, I was a successful and skilled business-focused HR practitioner—but I lacked a scientific foundation from which to build my thinking.

I began an even deeper exploration of the science of human behavior in the workplace when I joined The Work Institute. Following a very spirited lunch one day with "Dr. Tom," I had a revelation about many of the "truths" I had been taught and relied upon. Suddenly, traditional HR practices became all the more questionable.

The fact is, I practically ran back to my office and had the outline written for this book in just a few minutes.

Consider this book a casual guide to workforce research and employee surveys. These chapters are intended to challenge many of the longstanding beliefs you have been taught in a class or been sold by a consultant. The simple fact is that there is a better way to understand your employees' observations, preferences, expectations, and intents. And they are important.

Knowing them will help you build a better, more profitable company. Isn't that what it's all about?

Danny Nelms, MBA
SVP & Managing Director
The Work Institute

Introducing – The Server

I know a lot about you and your company. All day long I document and observe discussions between you and your fellow managers. I know what your consultants and employees are saying.

Hey—over here! Yes, I'm your company's network server. You know, the 6400, best-in-class? It's really me, and we need to have a serious talk.

I'm in a unique position. I'm an insider with insider information, a listener taking it all in. The stock market is up. The stock market is down. Unemployment is up and then unemployment is down. Corporate profits are up, but the pressure to do more with less is always present. The news is different every day, and leaders often have no idea what to pay attention to and what to do next.

Most of your employees like your company and their work. These employees genuinely want to do better and want your company to do better. Lately they've been talking about the things that are getting in the way of success.

I also know that many of your employees are actively looking for a new job. Others are planning on looking elsewhere as soon as the job market opens.

I expect I will miss them ... I know you will.

As a manager, you need to know what your employees are really thinking, what they are really planning. You need to know why they are thinking about leaving. You need to know what needs to be different so employees will want to stay longer. You also need to know what barriers need to be removed so employees can get more done, quicker.

I'm talking about the *real reasons*.

The fact is your employees know how easy it would be for you to improve your company—and most of the improvements don't require wasting company resources on the things you are currently doing. Mostly, improvement involves listening (*hearing* really) what your employees are saying, and then acting on what you learn.

When you sent out that recent survey, for instance, all I heard for days was, "It's a waste of time." Too many others said they weren't going to take it seriously. Some of the longer-term employees told the newer employees, "Oh, I've done lots of these and nothing changes." One guy said he'd been filling them out for ten years and has yet to get any feedback or see results based on what employees are thinking.

I've heard you say that you want your company to be the best, to be a place where people want to work, a place where they can do great work.

I believe you.

I also believe you are making some mistakes.

Now don't be alarmed. It's all fixable. We just need to use the right tools to get to the right information. The right information will help you make the decisions necessary to accomplish your objectives and improve your organization.

Let's look at a few of my observations and even a few of my questions. I think you'll learn a *lot*.

Evidence-Based Management

Executives routinely dose their organizations with strategic snake oil: discredited nostrums, partial remedies, or untested management miracle cures. In many cases, the facts about what works are out there – so why don't managers use them?

Jeffrey Pfeffer and Robert Sutton

What gets measured gets managed.

Peter Drucker

Here We Go Again

Yesterday was quite a day! E-mail traffic increased by 30 percent after the big all-employee meeting. I wondered what the buzz was about, so I actually started reading some of the e-mails.

I see your company is bringing in yet another group of consultants to tell you what to do.

One thing about servers is that we have long memories. By my count, this is the fourth group of consultants in the last five years brought in to improve productivity.

The scary part is that nothing has really ever changed. And your employees have basically the same expectations this time.

I listened in on the consulting group's debriefing report. They already have the road map in place to "fix" your productivity issues. So far, they have had two meetings with executive team members and have culled the financial reports and reviewed the benefit model. And they have a PowerPoint presentation ready to sell their solutions to your company.

You call that consulting?

How do they know your company is just like every other company they've sold their bill of goods to?

Please allow me to make a few observations.

These Are Serious Times That Require Serious Managers. Serious Managers Ask Serious Questions: How Do We Know We Need It? How Do We Know It Works?

Every decision your organization makes must be supported by data—sound and specific facts that guide improvements and eliminate errors.

It's called evidence-based management. It means you make confident, data-based, and knowledge-based decisions. It means you make decisions based on evidence. It means you operate out of the facts, not because you are enamored by the latest management best seller, a consultant's fancy sales pitch or someone else's (supposed) best practice.

- Fact: Most employees want to work for great companies.
- Fact: Most employees actually go to work every day wanting to do their best.
- Fact: Running great companies and doing great work are not easy. Many companies are actually pretty clueless as to how to manage this effectively.
- Fact: There's a lot of bad advice and a lot of bad tools out there.
- Fact: There are a lot of good tools but bad application.

Running great companies and making the right choices often boil down to this: How do you really know you need something, and how do you really know something works?

Well, your employees talk. Your customers talk. Your financials talk. Your leadership experiences talk. You just need a good mechanism for getting that information.

Your company is unique. Sure, it might share an industrial code, geography, and market with other companies. But your company is different. It has its own history, climate, organization, and identity. In many regards, your company is a living, breathing organism made up of the people who do the work that needs to be done.

Forget about the newest management trend. Hold at arm's length the new philosophy on training supervisors. Don't touch the benefit plan on the say-so of a self-serving adviser.

It's time to ask yourself if the so-called best practices you have put in place are actually the best at getting results. Is your pay-for-performance plan really improving performance? Is your wellness plan helping to improve the health of your employees, and your organization? Is your performance management system really improving the performance of your business?

It's time to consider the unique preferences, expectations, and intentions of your employees. Consider the fact that your best practices come from within your ranks and are specific to your company.

Employee versus Employer Marketplace

No matter how far you have gone down the wrong road, turn back.

Turkish Proverb

Traditional companies today have reached a decision point. It is at this point where they can choose to grow through responsible intelligence-based, value-based and ethics-based decision making -- or they can continue to operate as they do, thus taking the route of the dinosaur.

Thomas F. Mahan

Do You Think Your Company Is in Control?

Important articles are circulating around the office. It turns out that multiple studies are all saying the same thing. Across industry, geography, age, and profession, 50 percent of the workforce is either looking for another job or completely disengaged from their work. This thought definitely scares me. And it should scare you. If this data is representative of your company, this could mean half of your employees are not putting their hearts and minds into their jobs. And they will leave as soon as the opportunity presents itself.

- Is this true in your organization?
- Are people leaving?
- Are people increasingly disconnected?
- Are people planning on leaving?
- Is employee intent reflected in the quality of their work?
- How do you know?

I actually decided to take a little stroll through the HR department's history of turnovers and found some interesting stuff. Until the early 1990s, turnover was low and stayed about the same every year. Then things started to change. Slowly, turnover started to increase, and employees started to think differently about work, their relationship with their employers, and their career development.

Some of you are still pretty traditional in your thinking. You still view employees as dependents, content to work in the cocoon in return for decent pay, benefits, and a 401(k).

Actually, compensation and benefits, along with working conditions, supervision, and something called work-life balance, are key areas you keep asking employees to rate on surveys.

What is it that makes you believe these are the important areas for inquiry and remediation or development? If these are the questions you're asking employees, it follows that this is how you are (for some reason) defining the problem. If this is true, this is how you will attempt to solve the problem.

But what if these areas of inquiry and development are *not* representative of the real problems?

Employees Are in Control

Since the dawn of the industrial age until the 1990s, companies were more or less in control of the employment relationship. People went to work for a company and often remained there throughout their careers. People were loyal to their companies, and companies were loyal to their people.

Then a shift happened. Downsizings and layoff models violated the traditional employment contract and lifelong employee relationship. Companies went through cost-cutting and efficiency shifts, and notably, retirement plans and health insurance became portable. Employees came to realize they need not be dependent on a single employer to fulfill a lifelong employment contract, and they needed to manage their careers differently. This newly liberated employee population, this emerging workforce, recognized a way to achieve career satisfaction and opportunity by finding opportunities elsewhere.

Thus, the world of work continues to transition from an employer-in-control to an employee-in-control environment. This transition defines an emerging workforce, an employee population whose attitudes and preferences differ from the workforce of the past. It is in this new workforce that employee preferences and expectations continuously evolve in the areas of involvement and collaboration, technology integration, critical thinking, social networking, and innovation.

Today's employees have unique gifts—knowledge and skills—they will leverage. Both traditional and emerging employees will choose *where* and *how* to exercise their occupational and social purpose.

Some managers still talk about tough economic times and high unemployment as if the employer-in-control scepter has been put back in their hands, and they can rule the employees again. These companies and managers are ignoring the fact that the restricted opportunity job market will end. High unemployment and a subsequent compromise in attention to employees is a blip on the economic radar screen. Those who ignore this will lose.

Today's companies must know and respect employee preferences, expectations, and intents. And they must acknowledge this by communicating back to employees. Employees have a voice that must be heard. Unless you respect that voice, they *will* leave.

- To keep employees, maximize them.
- To maximize employees, listen to them.
- To listen to employees, hear them.
- To hear employees, care enough to believe they have much to offer.

They do. They will make your company better—and they will save you money.

Research Methodology —It Really Matters

The first rule of any technology used in a business is that automation applied to an efficient operation will magnify the efficiency. The second is that automation applied to an inefficient operation will magnify the inefficiency.

Bill Gates

Thanks to the Interstate Highway System, it is now possible to travel from coast to coast without seeing anything.

Charles Kuralt

What You Really Need to Know
(Or Do You Really Want to Know?)

So, I saw the e-bulletin announcing the launching of this year's employee satisfaction survey. Interestingly enough, it was a rewrite of last year's announcement. And like last year and the year before that, I saw the rolling eyes and heard the groans from the employees.

Some put off filling them out until the very last day, as usual, but some got right on it. They seemed to be completing them pretty quickly.

I've been listening to what they're saying about the survey. They're frustrated with the questions and the limits placed on their responses. Some just give up and quit the survey because they feel it doesn't let them provide real answers.

Lots of employees are bothered that the questions are self-serving to the company, basically reinforcing the management objectives that have little relevance to the employee population. Your employees are saying the questions are biased and force biased responses.

They have a point.

From what I see, you spend a lot of time on a survey that, if employees complete it at all, doesn't really provide the information you need to make responsible improvements. It seems your current survey method is built around administration, scoring convenience and benchmarking, rather than creating a way for you to get at the real issues.

Clearly, your survey is not getting at the truth.

The WHY Factor:
"Why" Is the Question that Really Matters

Good research methodology doesn't just tell you what needs improving; it tells you why, who, what, where, and how; and it gives you recommendations for improvement.

The only way to really get at what's going on in an organization is to use a mixed methodology, asking both qualitative and quantitative questions. The only way to get actionable intelligence is by opening up the opportunity for employees to answer questions and providing prompts that allow them to address their real concerns, preferences, expectations, intents, and recommendations. Open-ended questions require interviews, interviews that follow up with "why, what, who, where, and how" the respondent rated the item the way he or she did.

Ask current and former employees open-ended questions to secure the most comprehensive decision-making information possible.

While popular because they are affordable and easy to score, a fixed-scale response survey does not get at the real employee concerns and recommendations. Simply, paper-pencil, Interactive Voice Response (IVR), and internet data collection models do not work (more on these later). Data must be collected utilizing open-ended questions by skilled researchers who are able to establish rapport with your employees. (Consider the possibility that if a monkey could do it, it just might not be what you need.)

When asking an employee to rate items, such as how they view his or her supervisor, it is necessary to immediately follow up by asking why he or she chose that rating. A report full of statistics and not "real-world" responses can only tell you a fraction of what you really need to know to improve your work environment.

Here's what's really important: you deserve intelligence that guides and directs actionable remediation and development requirements.

Don't settle for less. You deserve the best, and the employee population definitely deserves it. Remember, a rating only tells part of the story. "Why" is the critical question.

Why Not Inside

As to methods there may be a million and then some, but principles are few. The man who grasps principles can successfully select his own methods. The man who tries methods, ignoring principles, is sure to have trouble.

Ralph Waldo Emerson

Trust Is Critical

Here's a scenario: lots of e-mails and memos are floating around about a certain manager who is boasting that he can name at least 90 percent of the respondents who made comments on his employee survey. How does he know? He recognizes the handwriting; he knows the way a certain employee talks. He also has a control document that helps him know who did and did not complete the survey. This guy is tracking his employees' responses.

I wonder if this will affect how he treats and evaluates the employees. I suspect it does. His employees believe it does.

If you were an employee of the bragging manager, would you fill out a survey if you thought it would put you at risk? Wouldn't you zip your lips if you figured he was listening in?

Reviewing, comparing and correlating some of my files also tells me that employees' complaints toward certain managers' behavior seem to regularly decrease just prior to survey time, year after year. I suspect that managers are "kinder" to employees just before survey time. This might have something to do with supervisor ratings.

Oh, another note just came through. It seems a department manager is reporting that she won't fill out the survey because she has to go in through the company computer and include a login number. She doesn't trust that it's anonymous and fears she would be punished for any unflattering responses.

The Objective Is to Get Good Data, Not Just Complete a Survey

Managers often don't realize that there is strategic information that can be secured from current talent, talent that has left the organization, and talent that is coming into the organization. If they really want the truth, managers can secure knowledge of what people are saying about the company and what the company is doing and not doing.

Let's face it: research science is clear that there is a correct way to conduct surveys. If you are serious about making improvements, you must utilize survey methods that guarantee comprehensive and safe reporting, and ask questions that get at the truth.

- Fact: Data collected inside often has questionable validity. Repeated studies have shown that data collected by inside sources yields very different results from data collected by outside, objective, third-party agents.
- Fact: Data collected from inside as opposed to outside, objective sources is often compromised and "dampened" to reflect a "let's-not-burn-the-bridge" mentality.
- Fact: The only way to ensure actionable intelligence is to conduct your research through an objective, outside, confidential, professional research organization.

Also, if your employees trust you and trust that you will actually act on the results they provide, they're much more likely to be honest. The more trust they have in you, the more likely they'll participate in the research. After all, it's in your company's best interest to have as many employees as possible participate in employee studies. The data is more accurate and ... well, you might as well get your money's worth.

Foster trust.

Trust encourages honesty.

The result is accuracy.

What you really want is a direct link to the hearts and brains of your employees without knowing whose bodies the data resides in.

Anonymity is critical to receiving accurate data, and compromising that anonymity limits the accuracy of employee responses.

Choose the Correct
Research Partner

For every complicated problem there is a simple solution
--- and it's wrong.

H.L. Mencken

Research Companies Are Not All the Same

Okay, the story is out that you are gearing up to do an employee survey. And the responses are flooding into my Request for Proposal (RFP) folder.

I'm WOWED on three counts:

- WOW: It seems that employee survey experts are crawling out of the woodwork. I didn't know there were so many behavioral scientists out there. Lots of consulting organizations are re-branding themselves and selling services beyond their level of training and expertise.
- BIGGER WOW: Lots of the responses seem to recommend an online data collection methodology. I know technology is helpful, but that doesn't mean it's the end-all, be-all solution. Somehow people think that just because the technology is there, it is "god"—I mean good.
- BIGGEST WOW YET: I'm getting a kick out of all the responses from companies that are primarily in the business of selling packaged solutions. Every one of their RFP responses suggest that they will not only do the study but will implement their packaged solutions. How can they claim to know what is needed prior to the study even being conducted? How can it be ethical to collect data and sell solutions?

They Want to Sell You Additional Services That Are Core to *Their* Business (Not Yours)

Companies make mistakes hiring solution providers to conduct employee and customer research. They hire consultants or survey companies that are not objective.

- If you hire a benefits company to come in and do your survey, guess what? You'll be changing your benefit programs.
- If you hire a compensation company to come in and do your survey, all your changes will be tied to a revised compensation program.
- If you hire a leadership development company to do your surveys, it looks like their recommendation will be a management- and supervisory-development program.

And on it goes.

What you're really doing is hiring people who already know what they're going to do. They sell programs. This isn't just your problem, it is a global one. Companies around the world are spending billions of dollars contracting with self-serving consultants.

If a consultant or survey company is in the business of selling services other than research, run—fast—in the other direction. You want to hire a company that is in the research-business only. That's who will provide unbiased intelligence.

Think of it in terms of medicine. If you have a pain in your stomach, would you go directly to a surgeon to have it operated on? No. You would go to a doctor who runs diagnostics and then makes an evidence-based recommendation for the proper intervention.

You want the same for your business.

Maybe, just maybe:

- Research is about strategy and solutions.
- Surveys are about selling programs.

Employee Engagement

A relationship, I think, is like a shark, you know? It has to constantly move forward or it dies. And I think what we got on our hands is a dead shark.

Woody Allen

The dominant societal power, whether it be religious, political or economic, propounds and directs self-serving myths because of its awareness that the stronger the belief in myths the easier it is to shape human behavior.

Frederick Herzberg

Is Employee Engagement Really the Magic Bullet?

So the top-line feedback from the annual survey was e-mailed to all managers today. Your company had an engagement score of 4.0 out of 5. Everybody is celebrating, and the communications department has come to life, drafting press release announcements to the population at-large.

I got a little curious, so I went back into my databanks and pulled the last three engagement surveys. One survey had sixty-four questions, another thirty-two, and this year's survey had twelve questions. They each presented an overall engagement score and even provided a benchmark against other companies.

I have to admit I'm a little confused. You see, even though 80 percent of employees were engaged, 30 percent of those engaged also indicated they would likely be leaving the company in less than a year. And with all these articles about employees looking for new jobs, these numbers simply don't compute. If an employee is really engaged, why is he or she looking for a new job?

Perhaps I just don't understand the term "engagement." (I actually thought it had to do with making a promise to marry.) There seem to be several definitions.

1. Current conceptualizations of engagement include attitudes such as satisfaction, commitment, involvement, loyalty, and empowerment.
2. Some companies are arguing that employee engagement is some kind of new behavioral science, a breakthrough if you will, that connects employee satisfaction to business outcomes.

3. Others are saying that employee engagement is just the latest buzzword and that it offers nothing different from the satisfaction and motivation surveys of the 1950s and '60s.

4. Some say engagement is merely a new brand—a way for consultants to sell last year's fashions at marked-up prices.

Employee Engagement Isn't What It's Cracked up to Be

If you asked ten consultants to define engagement, you will probably get ten different responses. If you ask how they will determine the engagement of your employee population, this is when it really gets fun. You see, there is no real science to back up a methodology for identifying engagement. Some consultants would even call engagement a myth. Nevertheless, without a clear and common definition, understanding and implementing solutions for engagement remain cluttered, scattered, and unfocused.

At The Work Institute, we don't try to dazzle our clients with fancy formulas for engagement, and we don't profess to know the exact twelve, thirty-two, or sixty-four questions that will identify an engaged employee.

There are five things we know to be true:

1. Employees know what they expect from an employer.
2. Employees know how they want to be treated by their supervisor.
3. Employees know how to create a better workplace.
4. If you create this better workplace, employees will stay for a long time, be more productive, be more innovative, and will create better relationships with your clients and customers.
5. Employee attitude and satisfaction drive customer satisfaction, and customer satisfaction drives organizational effectiveness, growth, and profitability.

The key to creating an engaged workforce is really pretty easy – *ASK, HEAR, AND ACT.*

Response Rates

Ends do not justify means, but rather means justify means, and means have a way of becoming ends, so it is well to be scrupulous and uncompromising as to means.

Albert Camus

You'd Better Know What 30 Percent Really Means

I just processed a company-wide urgent e-mail. You know, the ones with the little red flags.

It announced that the deadline for completing the annual survey is tomorrow.

Shortly thereafter I forwarded an e-mail from the HR leader to the CEO saying that only 30 percent of the employees had responded so far to the survey, and he didn't think too many more were going to get completed by tomorrow.

Then the HR leader said to the CEO, "But that's okay. Our consultant said he can work with those figures."

Well, maybe he can. But he shouldn't.

There Is a Science to Response Rates!

Accuracy in the measurement of attitude and subsequent behavior (or behavior and subsequent attitude) is essential to continuous improvement.

Included in accuracy is confidence that the data collected are representative of the population being measured.

Low response rates simply provide bad data. In order to have confidence in the solution recommendations, and thus ensure the success of the recommendations once implemented, response rates must exceed 50 percent. A low response rate critically affects identifying areas for improvement and puts one at risk of making erroneous decisions.

Target response rates must be set at 50 percent or higher in order to have confidence in the data. That means data that has fewer than a 50 percent response rate is not worth looking at.

You also have to know how your research company defines response rate. Many companies boast "participation" rates of 90 percent. Don't be fooled. Participation rate and response rate are different.

Participation rate is computed by dividing the number of completed interviews by the number of completed interviews plus the number of refusals. For example, assume a study of 1000 employees resulted in
  - 500 completes
  - 200 missing or incorrect phone numbers
  - 60 ineligible or deceased employees
  - 70 refusals or breakoffs
  - 140 call rule exhausted
  - 30 other

In this example, the participation rate is 500/(500 + 70) = 88%.

Raw response rate is computed by dividing the number of completes by the total number of people in the starting sample. Therefore, utilizing the example above, the raw response rate is 500/1000 = 50%.

Adjusted response rate is computed by dividing the number of completes by the total number of people in the starting sample minus the number of bad phone numbers and the number of ineligible/deceased employees. Thus, in the example above, the adjusted response rate is 500/(1000 – 200 – 60) = 68%.

Research shows that an adjusted response rate of 50% or higher is essential in establishing confidence that the results can be generalized to the population. The lower the adjusted response rate, the lower the confidence in the conclusions. When the adjusted response rate is much below 50%, reviewers are at risk of making erroneous decisions.

Acting on limited response rate data puts you at risk of intervening in the wrong area.

Higher response rates provide dramatically different results from small response rates.

So you want lots of responders in order to make sound decisions and to avoid making operational and cost mistakes.

Gather Data Using a Pulsing Model

We are responsible for the effects of our actions; and we are also responsible for becoming as aware as we can of these effects.

Rollo May

The greatest secrets are written on billboards.

Daniel Quinn

The Annual Survey—Really?

The data you need but often don't ask for confuses me.

All day long I'm pushing reports to your finance professionals in response to their needs to have company, region, department, product line, and service line performance data. Moment by moment, I send reports on compliance, sales, and expense.

I gather up-to-the-minute intelligence on waste and loss, inventory, outstanding and scheduled orders, accounts receivable, and assets value. I have current data on open positions, cost of labor, frequency of absenteeism, loss due to employee relations violations (some of you actually budget for it), and costs of accidents and injury.

Your executives demand constant up-to-date information to run the company. These decision-makers who handle the company's financial behavior know the company is a living, breathing, and constantly changing organism.

Your decision-makers use data to increase opportunity, resolve problems, and make regular midstream corrections.

My confusion is this:

- How can you run your organization—an organization dependent on employee skills, knowledge, and attitude—without continuous intelligence on your employees' perceptions, preferences, expectations, and intents?
- Aren't you understating the human factor by limiting your employee knowledge to an annual study?
- How can you have comfort and predict employee behavior without continuous employee intelligence?
- How can you make midstream corrections without midstream data?
- How can any organization believe that an annual study report is a valid representation of the organization?

It's Just Not a Big Deal

Entirely too many companies follow a tired tradition of doing an organization-wide survey every year or two. Often these same companies treat the survey as if it's a major strategic event. It's not. Data must be collected throughout the year so as to understand the evolving preferences, expectations, and intents.

Can you imagine if the accounting department treated your balance sheet as an annual major strategic event?

Just as the finance reports guide and direct the organization, so too employee intelligence, in a human dependent economy, must be collected, reported, and used to continuously guide change and innovation.

Current intelligence must be available 24/7.

- Within hours of obtaining information from employees, an organization's database must be updated and reports generated and delivered to decision-makers.
- Within seconds of obtaining information about a specific "flagged" issue (e.g., interest in being rehired, fraud, abuse, or illegal or unethical issues), e-mail alerts must be sent to designated representatives in the organization. Immediate follow-up is possible and often necessary.
- Intelligence must be tracked over time to evaluate the effectiveness of improvement efforts.

It's not complicated at all. Companies need to:

- Establish a baseline.
- Identify areas requiring critical focus.

- Implement evidence-based development and remediation requirements.
- Continuously update and track employee intelligence monthly based on $1/12^{th}$ of the population where possible.

Just like the demands of the executive office and the finance department, you too need to demand constant, up-to-date information. With timely and valid employee intelligence, you can define and execute your workforce performance objectives.

An annual report isn't up to date, neither is an annual survey. A two-week snapshot is not representative of what is really going on in the organization (except maybe during those two weeks).

Choose instead a Pulse Model. It works.

Employee Life Cycle

Can two walk together except they be agreed?

Amos 3:3

I not only use all the brains I have, but all that I can borrow.

Woodrow Wilson

Things Look Different on Day One, Day Ninety, and Day One Hundred Eighty

I want to show you a couple of e-mails that I have in storage—and one that came through today.

NOVEMBER:

Dear Bob: Just a short note to say thanks again for the networking assistance you provided me during my job search. I've been here for two weeks. All I can say is, this is a great place. Every day I am thankful for being able to work in a place like this.

Betty, my mentor and department head, is great. She has identified some challenging projects she wants me to own and has assured me that I will have the freedom and information necessary to get them done. I'm looking forward to it all. Employee relations are great. Can you believe they stock the lunchroom with beverages and occasional snacks? We can walk in and help ourselves.

I look forward to being here for a long time. Thanks again.

FEBRUARY:

Dear Bob: I trust you are well. I've been here about a hundred days now. There's still a lot that needs to be done around here. The projects I was brought in to do have basically been put on hold. Other critical (firefighting) things keep getting in the way. My project manager has changed twice since I've been here. They keep quitting. I hope it's not me (ha ha). Seriously, all these personnel changes are a bit frustrating, but I still feel positive. I think my boss is okay with my work, and I still believe we are in a good business, and given the opportunity, we can do some good things.

Anyway, thanks for your help last fall. I'll keep you posted.

TODAY:

Dear Bob: Hate to bother you with this but wonder if you might have time for a quick advise-and-counsel meeting. You were very helpful to me when I left my prior employer, and I think it's time to start looking at options again.

I've been here about six months and expect I will stay here through the end of the year (bonus is paid in December). Beyond that is doubtful. The climate around here is actually quite punishing. My boss is always mad at everyone (except the new employees, who she thinks love her). Basically, she brings me down. She is constantly nagging about all the projects that don't get done. The fact is she keeps chasing away the project team members.

Anyway, any chance of a long cup of coffee? This time it's my treat.

Managers Require Talent P&Ls, Talent Balance Sheets, and Talent Intent Prediction Statements

To make responsible decisions, executives depend on P&L statements (point in time reporting) and balance sheets (over-time reporting). Responsible and successful management requires that managers continuously assess how a company performs during periods, how it performs after the fact, and how it is likely to perform in the future.

Likewise, and especially in this human asset economy, managers can know employee observations, preferences, expectations, and intentions at any point in time and over time. Managers can also have a sense of employee intention regarding plans and timing to stay or leave and why they will stay and why they will leave.

- Managers must have the information necessary to understand and predict employee behavior at any point in time and over time.
- Managers must be able to assess and predict employees' intent to stay—especially critical employees' intent to stay.
- Managers must understand what needs to be done to reduce turnover and other manageable behavioral risks and expenses.

Depending on your requirements, The Work Institute recommends the following considerations for data collection and reporting:

Stay Research: It is increasingly critical to look at your intent to stay measures and recommendations in addition to other items supported by your business objectives. Workforce managers have the ability to be predictive in talent management planning.

- Who is thinking about leaving the organization? Why?
- Who intends to stay? For how long? Why?
- What changes can be made to increase the likelihood of employees staying?
- Would employees recommend the company as a good place to work?
- Do unethical practices or behaviors exist within the company? Where? What are they?
- What is the biggest complaint about the company? How can this be addressed?

Exit Research: All former employees (voluntary and involuntary terminations) should be assessed so managers understand why people leave and what needs to be different for people to stay. In most cases, managers should look at exited employee observations as representative of the employees who remain.

In addition to affirmatively identifying risk management liabilities, talent management requires that you know:

- What is causing talent to leave your company?
- Where is talent going when they leave?
- Would former talented employees work for your company again in the future?
- What it would take to get former employees to reconsider an employment relationship with your company?
- What factors would be most important in affecting a return to your company?

On-Board Research: On-boarding and new-hire analyses provide valuable information regarding the preferences and expectations of new hires that companies can use to improve retention rates.

- When do new hires begin to consider leaving? How does the company cause this to occur?
- What expectations do new hires have regarding their job? Is the organization meeting them?
- Are new hires' expectations aligned with the company's expectations for them?
- What are new hires' primary or most common complaints about the company? How and where can interventions resolve this issue?
- What do new hires recommend the company do in order to improve the on-boarding experience?

Recruiting Effectiveness: Are there people standing in line to work at your organization? You can develop *competitive advantage* in your industry and geography by learning what attracts applicants to rival organizations and what discourages applicants from choosing your organization.

Recruitment and attraction studies provide critical information relating to the preferences, expectations, and intents of your applicant base. Understanding the preferences and expectations of your applicants is crucial to enhancing your attraction strengths and remedying your attraction weaknesses.

- Why are people choosing to apply at your organization?
- Why are people not choosing to apply at your organization?
- Where else are your applicants choosing to apply? Why?
- If applicable, why didn't he or she accept your offer?
- Can you get these applicants to reconsider your company? How?

- How did the applicant hear about your company and the job?
- How did the applicant feel about your company's recruiting and application process?
- What would the applicant recommend as ways to improve your recruitment?

Responsibly collected employee life-cycle data are evaluative and predictive. They tell you how well you've done as an employer and what needs to be done to meet your human asset goals in the future.

Scoring for Actionable Results

If I had eight hours to chop down a tree, I'd spend six sharpening my ax.

Abraham Lincoln

Manipulating Data

You know, I process data 24/7 and make it available to you whenever you call for it. Sure, I'm quick (if I'm taken care of), but the fact is, I stay simple—I only manage 0s and 1s.

I like rules. Rules provide some order and stability and actually keep things pretty simple. Two-plus-two always equals four; assets are in black; liabilities are in red; e-mails have @s; locations have .coms, .nets, and .orgs; and cold is on the right and hot is on the left.

But as I've previously mentioned, you humans confuse me. You know I processed the data reports from your research company. I saw the questions and the analysis and the scoring.

I also saw all the e-mail correspondence about how you plan to report the scores. Your plan doesn't compute, as it doesn't follow the rules of math.

The way the satisfaction with management data came in reflected the following scale:

Poor	Fair	Good	Very Good	Excellent
17%	22%	46%	12%	3%

Why did you combine the fair, good, very good and excellent scores and then report that 83 percent of employees are satisfied with management? Don't you want to report things as they really are? Won't misinterpreting and misreporting the data cause you to spend money intervening in the wrong area? Won't it cause a lack of trust between those who completed the survey and those who interpreted the findings? Couldn't this manipulation of the data actually hasten the exit of employees?

Accuracy in Scoring

Research methodology and scoring (and reporting) must create intelligence for companies to determine actions for improvement—and evaluate the effectiveness of those actions. As such, responsible research includes rating scales and probes to find out why the specific rating was given.

Understanding a scale, how it presents, and how it is interpreted is important for data analysis and reporting.

Rating scale questions (e.g., Excellent, Very Good, Good, Fair, and Poor) are interpreted first by focusing on the combined percentage of respondents who give a Fair or a Poor rating (the bottom two ratings combined).

If the combined percentage of Poor and Fair ratings for a question is 15 percent or higher, the topic of the question must be considered a priority concern and an area for improvement—the higher the percentage of combined Fair/Poor, the higher the priority. Employees who give these ratings are usually angry and risk spreading negativism to others.

If there are no questions with a combined percentage of Fair/Poor ≥ 15 percent, the focus can move to the top of the rating scale (e.g., percent Excellent). The Excellent rating is indicative of employees who are delighted.

Critical note: Sometimes organizations will report the percentages of Excellent and Very Good combined, or even the percentages of Excellent, Very Good, Good, and Fair combined. This may work for public relations and recruiting purposes, but doing so is merely denying a problem. Ignoring problem areas will continue to compromise organizational effectiveness.

Priorities for improvement include:

- Areas with % Fair/Poor > 15%
- Areas with % Fair/Poor <15% but with % Excellent < 30%
- Areas with % Fair/Poor <15% and % Excellent between 30% and 50%

Once percentages have been used to identify priorities for improvement, the *"Why"* reasons for the ratings can help determine what to do.

Reporting: It's Your Data

Genius is only a superior power of seeing.

John Ruskin

You'd Better Know the Deal Upfront

"She" worked on your proposal for days. It was the final response to your Survey Request for Proposal (RFP).

She's good. I've seen her in action over the years. Hers is a customized, top-quality research company.

- She answered all your questions, identified your objectives, and made sure the designed and tested questionnaire addressed areas regarding your company's specific improvement opportunity. She made suggestions that clearly and responsibly enhanced your outcome opportunity.
- She identified in advance every report you would need, broken down by the variables you said were important—and then some.
- She constructed a way to immediately release your reports, even though the RFP anticipated a three-month reporting period.

Today, your e-mail response arrived. She lost the bid. Your purchasing department opted to go with the (apparently) lower-cost bidder.

But the low bid is misleading. The low-ball bidder is notorious for later adding on services. Expensive reports and deeper dives into the research are sure to be added as an addendum to the original agreement.

She stared down at her latte and mimicked one of the competing consultants. "Oh, you want that data broken down into job categories? We can do that for you. I'll give you an estimate.

"That's just the beginning," she predicted. "They'll be doing that for years. It will cost them three times what we bid!"

You Have Ratings Data, but Is It Sufficient for Knowing What to Do?

It happens every day. Consultants enter your company with promises of getting your survey done. They low-bid the study, and you think you have negotiated a great deal.

You are right on schedule! The data were collected on time, the response rate is adequate, and the .pdf reports are being distributed. Time to celebrate a job well done!

Let's go over the reports. It seems you have lots of ratings data, but unfortunately, this data is insufficient for explaining exactly what the ratings mean. You don't have enough information to determine an evidence-based solution.

So let's fix it. The consultant is recommending something called Focus Groups. Don't worry, the consultant will facilitate and report on these groups for you. After all, this is one of their core competencies. You only need to pull your people away from productive behavior, send out the memos, and schedule the meetings. Oh, and soda and snacks would be helpful. It's really no big deal in the grand scheme of things—it will only extend the project timeline a month. Certainly the executive team will understand the extension in schedule and the increase in cost. Won't they? Good thing you have the time.

Oh, and now you want additional reports? The consultants will need to charge you for all the different reports. After all, they're outside the scope of their response to your proposal. Seems they didn't know you wanted reports broken down by age, sex, location, job role, EEO codes, performance rankings. They didn't know you would want to look at other variables, such as succession planning categories (although they should have predicted these wants).

And so it goes. It's almost predictable.

Want some advice? When you're getting quotes regarding research, make sure you have a full and complete understanding of what the data reports will look like. Get samples.

Also, verify that you have full and complete access to the data. Nobody owns your data but you. Your employees provided it, and you paid for it. Don't keep paying a consulting company to have it sliced, diced, and resold to you. Make sure reports are available and accessible to you at all times.

Intelligence to Action

There's no difference between the pessimist who says, "oh, it's hopeless, so don't bother doing anything," and an optimist who says, "Don't bother doing anything, it's going to turn out fine anyway." Either way, nothing happens.

Yvon Chouinard

Once a problem is well understood, an elegant solution is possible.

Unknown

You Must Know What's Next

I've been processing your data for years now. I've seen project plans developed and managed, and I've seen projects fall by the wayside. As it relates to your annual survey plans, mostly what I see is lots of activity in the collection but no activity following the reports.

My logic systems have me questioning why you do a survey at all. Sure, I expect you have good intentions. Why else would you spend so much money on the survey?

Here's how it usually goes:

- You select the low cost provider.
- Someone in HR chooses a survey launch day.
- The surveys are completed and collected.
- Then things get really slow. The data is analyzed, and a report is made.
- The report goes to a "survey committee," and additional information will likely be required.
- Perhaps focus groups are conducted because the data you collected in your quantitative-only study didn't provide the necessary information.
- Eventually, it all goes to the leadership team, who looks at it and decides what to share (or not share) with the rest of the company.
- Usually by the time it's ready to be shared, a year has gone by and the company decides it needs another survey because this one is probably obsolete. The workforce hears nothing and has seen no change. And the next time a survey comes around, employees either don't complete it at all, or they rush through it, giving mostly negative feedback based on their frustrations.

Sound familiar?

Research Must Lead to Evidence-Based Action

It makes no sense to collect data about or from employees (current employees, former employees, applicants, and special populations) across the career life span for the sake of collecting data.

Research projects must be aimed at company objectives, not just at fulfilling historical practices ("but this is how we have always done it").

Research must answer business questions. For example, what must we do:

- To increase intent to stay, especially with our most talented and critical people?
- To reduce turnover?
- To increase our ability to recruit effectively?
- To anchor critical talent during mergers, acquisitions, and major changes?
- To improve productivity: the output value (revenue) relative to costs (labor, raw material, and equipment) of achieving that output?
- To proactively identify and manage fraud, abuse, and illegal or unethical behavior?

Action follows data. Intelligent data provides intelligent action. Bad data drives erroneous actions.

A good spy movie never ends with the agents capturing the intelligence; it starts with it. Good intelligence makes for a good, action-filled plot. It should do the same in your workplace.

Ask your employees for their observations, preferences, expectations, and intentions in order to create an environment where recommendations can be acted upon. For example, perhaps your top computer tech is considering leaving the company. What would it take on your part for her to stay? What are some of the conditions currently in the organization that are compromising her ability to perform?

Collect data that provide actionable intelligence to diagnose, prescribe, and evaluate the effectiveness of efforts designed to improve the return on investment (ROI) of human capital.

Human Capital Costs

It does not pay to leave a dragon out of your calculations if you live near him.

J.R.R. Tolkien

But What about the Human Capital Financials?

Do you know how many e-mail addresses, employee passwords, payroll classifications, health, life, and disability codes, 401(k) models, recruitment codes, and SSI, EEO, and employee ID numbers go through my system on a daily basis?

In fact, I am constantly processing applicant, new hire, current, and former employee data. I archive this data, and the ratio of employee codes I manage is close to ten times the number of people employed here.

A lot of what happens around here is hard for me to compute. For example, I also constantly process data on loss and waste, inventory control, and billing control. I know what the waste is on the production floor; I know what the ratio is between employee theft and shoplifting; and I know the areas where billing is missed (and where people are being billed for services not provided).

I regularly calculate and report the dollars lost and am aware of your process-improvement initiatives and the financial value of the controls you have put in place to curb these costs and improve productivity— those that relate to product and service assets, anyway.

But there is something that doesn't calculate for me. You do a great job at measuring for evidence-based intervention in the loss and waste, inventory control, and billing arena, but I don't see any attention on managing the controllable costs related to the people that do the work—your human behavior costs. Why not?

Here's some math: If you have a turnover rate of 25 percent in a company with six thousand employees, at a cost of $15,000 per person, what would your savings be if you reduced that to 20 percent, 15 percent, or even 10 percent?

That's real savings.

As You Intervene in the Manageable Human Asset Expense Area, You Have the Opportunity to Directly Influence the Company's Productivity

The Work Institute's Human Capital Financial Reporting (HCFR) service provides a way for organizations to understand specific manageable human costs and set objectives for reducing those costs. Securing accurate HCFR intelligence is critical for any organization to operate at its highest efficiency level. With this intelligence, leaders can identify specific cost-saving objectives and measure the success of these objectives over time.

Costs measured include:

- Hiring Costs & Trends
- Absenteeism Costs & Trends
- Employee Turnover Costs & Trends
- Safety Violation Costs & Trends
- Unemployment Insurance Costs & Trends
- Employee Utilization of Pretax Benefits
- Workers Compensation Costs & Trends
- Employee Relations Cost & Trends
- Fraud/Unethical Risk Incidents Costs & Trends
- Shrinkage/Theft Cost & Trends
- Agency Costs
- Other Related Costs Unique to the Client

With this intelligence, companies can make evidence-based decisions about which areas make the most sense (financially) to prioritize. Understanding such information provides the business case for responsible and financially advantageous intervention.

You can have specific and timely research that can identify strengths and weaknesses in the human-behavior arena. You can have employee observation, preferences, expectation, and intent intelligence that can drive cost effective evidence-based intervention, just like in the product and service arena.

From the Server

Make everything as simple as possible, but not simpler.

Albert Einstein

I'm glad we had this opportunity to talk. I love the fact that my observations continue to amaze, even in a server capacity.

You need to go back and amaze that executive management team with what you have learned. Tell them about evidence-based management and its importance in the decision-making process. Remind them that 50 percent of your organization is at risk of being disengaged—and many of your employees could be looking for new jobs. Tell them not to alarm them but to identify a real and growing issue that needs to be addressed. It is also a great opportunity for cost savings.

Also, remind the managers that regardless of temporary shifts in the unemployment market, it remains an employee-in-control marketplace, so you need to acquire the intelligence to learn what your employee population is thinking. Remember the "WHY" factor: you need intelligence that guides and directs your actionable opportunities. You need to understand what is affecting employee behavior, their likes, dislikes, and intent to stay or leave.

Most important, use this intelligence to take positive action. Make improvements where the data is identifying problem areas. Expand the processes where the data shows you are yielding positive results.

In closing, remember this last point: I am here to serve. I work hard at it, and that's what allows me to amaze. Now, to successfully implement your actionable plan, remind everyone that the best leaders are those who serve.

Afterword

Let's face it, as a rule most companies still struggle to recognize the value of people. We keep talking about "people as our greatest asset," and yet we often continue treating our talent base as a commodity – to be used up, disposed of, and (if available and affordable) replenished.

Where unemployment is high and companies are not growing as fast as they would like, employee value may not be at the forefront. However, as unemployment goes down and companies and markets choose to grow, employee value and the proper management of employee value will be a requirement.

Recent studies tell us that as many as 50% of today's employees are looking to change jobs when they become available. The question remains: Is your company prepared for this eventuality? Do you know what your employee intent is? As the economy recovers, will you succeed at keeping the key employees who will be able to find the jobs they want?

Most organizations continue to be in denial that many of their key employees are, as we breathe, thinking about leaving. The scary reality is that based on all the stresses on our workforces over the past couple of years, you may not even know the real issues causing employees to want to leave your company.

As a veteran executive with over 20 years of experience, I can tell you this is like driving an organization with a blindfold!

If we are to be strategic in our roles as leaders, then we must know that attracting and retaining the best talent is the one job we cannot afford to fail. The simple truth is the unwanted turnover of key talent has the potential to kill companies financially. Along with disengagement, absenteeism and the loss of productivity that precede it, turnover robs (and will continue to rob) companies of financial value, by increasing human capital costs.

The good news is that there is an evidenced based approach to understanding the many issues affecting your workforce. Unfortunately companies keep doing many of the same erroneous things, utilizing popular (but not proven) solution attempts without ever having the evidence to back it up. A strategic approach (and the win) to the attraction and retention of employees is to secure knowledge about what people are saying about the company, and what the company is doing and not doing effectively.

The vast majority of employee feedback mechanisms in use today are on-line, fill in the dot, survey tools. Although these tools may reveal information, they most often don't uncover the real reasons why employees (or customers) will choose to leave or stay with an organization, and they do not uncover the actionable data that must be gathered.

The Work Institute specializes in comprehensive customized workforce research gathered through a unique telephonic interview. This behavioral interview is conducted by asking some broad open-ended questions that allow employees to report the issues that are important to them, and gathers the qualitative information necessary to identify the issues affecting employees' intents and expectations. We then provide this information to client companies via a proprietary reporting tool (Human Asset Vulnerability Analysis—HAVA) that allows unlimited access to the critical information employees are sharing about the organization and the employment relationship.

While quantitative surveys may provide you a compass to understand direction, The Work Institute methodology is a GPS! We can hone in on the key actionable information so you drive your organization and achieve your goals with confidence

Danny Nelms

Frequently Asked Questions

How can we combine the richness of qualitative data with the specificity of quantitative data?

"Tele-research" is a great vehicle for obtaining responsible and rich reporting. Your tele-research provider must be committed to ensuring that researchers are fully capable of dealing with employees across organizational levels. The ability of the researcher to quickly establish trust and rapport with former and current employees is critically important to the quality of the final product. The researchers must be skilled in behavioral interviewing, including listening, hearing, and asking appropriate follow-up questions. They also must understand the importance of anonymity and confidentiality.

What response rate is okay?

High adjusted response rates (around 50 percent) are essential to be able to trust interview data. Calculate adjusted response rates by dividing the number of completed surveys by the total number of employees minus the number of incorrect phone numbers.

What is the business case for employee research?

Employee research in today's work environment is clearly a return-on-investment (ROI) strategy. The compelling case for responsible employee research is that there are human capital costs that can be managed, reduced, and eliminated.

An additional business case for employee research includes companies' ability to focus on the value of understanding why people are joining, staying, and leaving and why they would or wouldn't work for the organization again. This intelligence clearly provides insight into what the organization is doing to attract, keep, and drive people away. Also, the ability to track reasons over time provides valuable ROI intelligence on the effectiveness of efforts to improve.

What is the typical length of an employee tele-research interview?

Ten to fifteen minutes per interview.

How do I provide assurances of anonymity to our employees?

Stress the fact that you have a third party collecting the data and that their responses will be grouped with others before they are fed back to your organization (stressing anonymity). In addition, stress that your objective is to become a better employer and that you need employee help in defining what the company could do to meet this objective.

How do I estimate turnover cost and risk?

Turnover cost is based on four factors. These include the cost of termination, the cost of replacement, the vacancy cost (number of days job is open times the average value of the job per day [revenue/employee/day]), and learning curve (productivity) loss (revenue per employee per day times number of days it takes to get the new hire up to standard performance).

While these costs can be accurately calculated using specific formulae, it is often just as valuable to determine costs based on a *conservative short-cut procedure*:

Estimate mean annual "salary" cost for the position(s) being investigated $_____

Multiply by .33 (Dept. of Labor) $_____

Multiply by number of terminations in last 12 months

Annual Turnover Cost/Baseline = $_____

Glossary of Key Terms

Actionable Intelligence

Data gathered from a targeted population that is sufficiently rich and descriptive to direct actions that can be taken to change behaviors or the environment.

Annual Survey

The traditional, once per year method used to solicit employee feedback typically done on-line, via Interactive Voice Response or by filling out a paper survey tool. These models usually allow only for fixed scale response and (occasionally) limited comments.

Baseline

Taking measures to establish a starting point. In the case of workforce research, this involves establishing the initial ratings and perceptions of the population from which improvement can be measured over time.

Benchmark

Benchmarking is the process of comparing one's business processes or performance metrics to others in the industry or geography and/ or best practices from other organizations.

Closed-ended questions

Closed-ended questions can take many forms, but the most common types are ratings (e.g., Excellent, Very Good, Good, Fair, Poor), agreement (e.g., Strongly Agree, Agree, Disagree, Strongly Agree and Yes/No/Maybe), importance (e.g., Very Important, Important, Somewhat Important, Not Important), frequency (e.g., Often, Sometimes, Seldom, Never). These types of questions have in common the requirement that very specific statements need to be presented for evaluation, agreement, determining importance, or assessing frequency. A problem with closed-ended questions is that the respondent is forced to react to specific questions rather than identify the most salient issues.

Continuous Improvement

The process whereby a baseline is established and strategies and on-going measures are put into practice to assess and report positive changes over time.

Critical Talent

Employees whose skills, knowledge, licenses, certification, competencies, and (most importantly) contributions would be difficult or expensive to replace if the employee left the organization.

Emerging Workforce

Describes the transition from an employee who has limited choices and is dependent on an employer for work to an employee who takes ownership of their career and has the ability to makes choices to stay or leave an employer. Emerging workers typically are more concerned with gaining new experiences and having opportunities. They are more in control of their careers and want an employer that rewards them according to their contribution. Traditional workers, on the other hand, are more concerned with job security, stability and clear direction. They depend on the employer for providing a career path.

Employee Engagement

An "engaged employee" is one who is fully involved in, and enthusiastic about their work, and thus will act in ways that further their own and the organization's interests.

Employee-In-Control

Used to describe the work environment wherein employees have the ability and intent to determine where they want to work and the conditions in which they want to satisfy their occupational purpose.

Employer-In-Control

Used to describe the work environment wherein the employer is in primary control of the work relationship with employees. In this environment, employees have limited options and often must tolerate adverse work situations

Evidenced Based Management

An emerging management practice that asks and answers two specific questions: How do I know I need it? And how do I know it works? In an evidence-based environment, actions are taken only when the outcome of such action is specifically aligned with the data collected. Evidenced Based Management applies the scientific method to management practice.

Exit Research

Gathering critical information from former employees as a means to identify the real reasons the employee left the organization and determining the strengths and opportunities for improvement of the organization. Exit research, when done properly, can identify the real reasons why people left. Exit research can also serve to understand the real reasons why current employees are likely to leave.

Fixed Scale Response Survey

The most common employee survey tool. Employee answer options are limited to specific responses (e.g., Poor, Fair, Good, Very Good, or Excellent). Fixed Scale Response Surveys do not allow for explanation of the reasons for the selected response.

Focus Groups

A focus group is a form of qualitative research in which a group of people are asked about their perceptions, opinions, beliefs and attitudes regarding a variety of topics regarding an organization. Focus groups are often used to secure additional clarification of data collected in a fixed response survey method and answers are often biased by the facilitator and the most active responders.

Human Capital Financial Reporting

Increasingly, organizations are recognizing the importance of managing the costs of human capital. Human Capital Financial Reporting provides a way for identifying, measuring and costing key human capital metrics within an organization.

Human Dependent Economy

A way of describing a world-of-work that is dependent on human skills, knowledge and attitudes.

Interactive Voice Response Method

A means of data collection that utilizes a phone system with a pre-recorded script and data collection technology to complete a survey.

Internet Data Collection

A method of data collection that utilizes web-based tools to complete a survey.

Involuntary Termination

Involuntary termination is the employee's departure at the hands of the employer typically for cause, layoff, or a reduction in force.

Mixed Methodology

The research method which integrates the collection of quantitative and qualitative data.

On-Board Research

Gathering critical information from employees during the on-boarding phase of their employment (typically 60-180 days) as a means to identify the strengths and opportunities for improvement of the attraction and recruitment process as well as the organization in general.

Open Ended Questions

Questions which give the person answering the opportunity to fully respond to a question or inquiry. Open-ended questioning, done properly, provides qualitative responses. Open-ended questions have the advantage of eliciting those issues that are most salient to the respondent. If compensation is important, it will emerge. If it is not important, it won't. However, even more importantly, in open-ended questions respondents will say things like "I wasn't willing to keep doing this kind of work given the amount of money they are paying me," or "They expect too much work for the money they pay," or "People who do nothing get more money than I do," or "I got an offer that was just too good in terms of pay to turn down." If a pattern emerges that centers around better pay elsewhere, you would take different kinds of action than if the pattern that emerges has to do with asking too much for too little. Since responses to open-ended questions result in more actionable data, data collection methods must maximize the use of open-ended responses.

Productivity

Productivity is a ratio of what is produced to what is required to produce it. Usually this ratio is in the form of an average, expressing the total output divided by the total input.

Pulsing Model

Pulsing Model is the employee survey practice of soliciting employee feedback throughout a period of time, typically a year. Generally the employee population is broken into 1/12ths or 1/4ths and those employees are interviewed monthly or quarterly.

Recruitment Research

Gathering critical information from employees regarding the recruitment process as a means to identify the strengths and opportunities for improvement of the on-boarding process as well as the organization in general. Recruitment research can be conducted with both those that accepted as well as those that declined the offer to join an organization.

Request for Proposal (RFP)

The act of requesting that several organizations provide a proposal to complete specific work in the organization. The response to an RFP is often referred to as a Response to Proposal.

Research

Research can be defined as the search for information, with an open mind, to establish facts, solve new or existing problems, prove new ideas, or develop new theories.

Response Rates (Participation, Response and Adjusted Response Rates)

Some research firms confuse Response Rate terms. Three different response rates are addressed:

1. Participation Rate
2. Raw Response Rate
3. Adjusted Response Rate

Participation rate is computed by dividing the number of completed interviews by the number of completed interviews plus the number of refusals. For example, assume a study of 1000 employees resulted in

- 500 completes
- 200 missing or incorrect phone numbers
- 60 ineligible or deceased employees
- 70 refusals or breakoffs
- 140 call rule exhausted
- 30 other

In this example, the Participation Rate is 500/(500 + 70) = 88%.

Raw response rate is computed by dividing the number of completes by the total number of people in the starting sample. Therefore, utilizing the example above, the raw response rate is 500/1000 = 50%.

Adjusted response rate is computed by dividing the number of completes by the total number of people in the starting sample minus the number of bad phone numbers and the number of ineligible/deceased employees. Thus, in the example above, the adjusted response rate is 500/(1000 – 200 – 60) = 68%.

Research shows that an adjusted response rate of 50% or higher is essential in establishing confidence that the results can be generalized to the population. The lower the adjusted response rate, the lower the confidence in the conclusions. When the adjusted response rate is much below 50%, reviewers are at risk of making erroneous decisions.

Revenue

Revenue is income that a company receives from its normal business activities, usually from the sale of goods and services to customers.

Stay Research

Gathering critical information from current employees regarding their intent to stay and the conditions that must be present to increase the likelihood of staying longer.

Tele-Research

Utilizing trained behavioral interviewers to conduct research over the phone.

The Work Institute

A workforce research company based in Brentwood, TN.

Turnover Rate

The rate at which an employer gains and loses employees.

Voluntary Termination

An employee's decision to leave a job of his or her own accord.

About the Authors

Danny Nelms is the SVP and managing director at The Work Institute. Danny is a twenty-year veteran in human capital management with industry experience that includes professional services, manufacturing, and healthcare. Danny is an adjunct faculty member at Lipscomb University and has spoken on numerous occasions regarding workforce research and human capital management. Danny earned his Bachelor of Business Administration from Georgia State University in Atlanta, Georgia, and completed his MBA from the Massey School at Belmont University in Nashville, Tennessee.

Dr. Thomas F. Mahan is founder and chairman of The Work Institute, LLC. Prior to founding The Work Institute in 2000, Dr. Mahan was a senior vice president with the Saratoga Institute, a director of organization development with Cigna, and a general manager with Prentice-Hall. Professor Mahan, as time allows, lectures at Peabody College of Vanderbilt University. Dr. Mahan is also well-known through his teaching and conference speaking with national and international organizations. Tom is an executive career counselor and advisor, noted speaker, behavioral consultant, and author.

The Work Institute, LLC, a workforce intelligence company, empowers leaders to strengthen business, increase revenue, and reduce expenses by identifying improvement opportunities within organizations. Our comprehensive research solutions help organizations understand what drives employee and customer behavior. We collect and analyze data, emphasizing quantitative and qualitative responses to ensure that you not only know *what* people think and do—you know *why*.

Interested in Learning More About Workforce Research?

The Work Institute is a leader in relevant workforce and workplace research that provides decision support intelligence to help companies attract, hire and retain talent, improve performance, diminish risk and manage human capital cost.

The Work Institute's Employee in Control Interview Model uses a combined quantitative and qualitative probing question model designed to capture the most relevant and actionable data. This question design is structured to provide a basis for measurement, to elicit information that is important to the respondent, and to explore reasons and alternatives. Rating scale responses and verbatim comments are collected to provide a sound evidence basis for decisions and actions for improvement.

Results are immediately available to managers' at their desktops. The ability to continually track potential, new, current, and former employee observations, preferences, expectations and intentions over time provides valuable insights into how the organization can improve performance and competitiveness.

Services include:

- *Recruitment Effectiveness Research*
- *On-Boarding Studies*
- *Stay Research*
- *Exit Research*
- *Other Customized Research*

- *Customer and Patient Satisfaction*
- *Student Retention Studies*
- *Pre and Post Merger Analysis*
- *Leadership Assessments*
- *Supervisor Scorecards*

Understanding your employees' preferences, expectations, and intents is essential to eliminating the high cost of turnover, the expensive process of recruiting new hires, and the major issues that lead to dissatisfaction at the workplace.

Most survey companies focus on conducting annual or bi-annual engagement or satisfaction surveys. The reality is that employees' views change during the employment life-cycle. Their response after 30 days may be quite different than after two years. It is important to collect valuable intelligence from employees at varying times throughout the employment experience.

The Work Institute, based in Brentwood, Tennessee and operations in Florida, Illinois and Sao Paulo, Brazil, services customers in 17 countries, conducting research in 14 different languages.

The Work Institute
1620 Westgate Circle, Suite 100
Brentwood, TN 37027
Phone - 888.750.9008
workinstitute.com

Index

CPSIA information can be obtained at www.ICGtesting.com
Printed in the USA
LVOW110710020312

271218LV00001B/2/P